1 MONTH OF
FREE
READING

at

www.ForgottenBooks.com

By purchasing this book you are eligible for one month membership to ForgottenBooks.com, giving you unlimited access to our entire collection of over 700,000 titles via our web site and mobile apps.

To claim your free month visit:

www.forgottenbooks.com/free614992

ISBN 978-0-483-14959-5
PIBN 10614992

This book is a reproduction of an important historical work. Forgotten Books uses
state-of-the-art technology to digitally reconstruct the work, preserving the original format
whilst repairing imperfections present in the aged copy. In rare cases, an imperfection in
the original, such as a blemish or missing page, may be replicated in our edition. We do,
however, repair the vast majority of imperfections successfully; any imperfections that
remain are intentionally left to preserve the state of such historical works.

A

VIEW

OF THE

RELATIVE STATE

OF

GREAT BRITAIN

AND

FRANCE,

AT THE

COMMENCEMENT OF THE YEAR

1796.

London:

Printed for J. DEBRETT, opposite Burlington-House, Piccadilly.

1796.

A

VIEW

OF THE

RELATIVE STATE, &c.

IF ever there was a period in the hiſtory of mankind, when men of every deſcription, whoſe talents can conduce to ſupport the glory, or to promote the felicity of their country, are called upon to exert them in the public ſervice, the preſent is unqueſtionably the moment. The ſpirit of the age in which we live, and the events with which we are familiar, bear neither reſemblance,

nor

nor analogy to thofe of former times. Within little more than fix years, fince the origin of the French Revolution, we have feen all the land marks erected by human wifdom, and all the inftitutions rendered facred from antiquity, or venerable from prefcription, torn up and trampled under foot. The moft extravagant theories, and the wildeft metaphyfical fubtleties have been fubftituted in the place of experience, by men profeffing to exercife the functions of legiflation. Religion has been folemnly dethroned, to make way for the pretended reign of reafon. Rebellion and regicide have been declared facred and inalienable duties. Not only the forms of monarchical authority, and all the intermediate orders between the crown and the people, have been abrogated : the ties of marriage, upon which reft the foundations of focial union, and all the principles of fubmiffion, order, and morals, have been either indirectly at-

tacked

tacked with the keeneft fhafts of ridicule,
or demolifhed with open violence.

The powers of language, vaft and capa-
cious as they are, fink in the attempt to
defcribe the confequences and calamities
produced by the revolution of France. The
barbarians who in the decline of the Roman empire, over-ran and defolated all the
provinces, from the frontiers of Scandina-
via and Sarmatia, to the extremities of
Lufitania and Gaul, effected, it is true, a
total alteration, civil, political, and religi-
ous. They gave the laft blow to the ex-
piring fuperftitions of antiquity. They
erected new governments, on the ruins of
the old, adapted to their prejudices, their
convenience, or their neceffities. They
converted into a temporary defert, the moft
opulent, fertile, and populous countries of
Europe. But, here, at leaft, their deftructive ravages terminated. They did not,

like

like the French, endeavour to poifon and contaminate the fources of human felicity; to involve future times in perpetual difcord; and by promulgating doctrines of imaginary and impracticable equality, incompatible with fubordination, to render the earth itfelf only an immenfe theatre of diforder, crimes, and anarchy.

If the infular pofition of Great Britain, the vigour of the Englifh navy, the general diffufion of property, the good fenfe characteriftic of the nation, and the affectionate reverence, entertained for a conftitution and laws, which preclude injuftice and promote general happinefs, as far as the imperfection attached to man will admit; if thefe combined caufes have hitherto preferved us from imbibing the moral infection, who can, neverthelefs, undertake to promife for futurity? The inferior claffes, habituated to the confideration and difcuf-

fion

fion of fubjects, far beyond the limited range of their capacities, deluded by the example of France, and ftimulated by factious or unprincipled demagogues, may not always be withheld by the reftrictions which have operated on their predeceffors. The difeafes of the mind, like thofe of the body, are in fome meafure contagious. Adventitious and local circumftances may aid or accelerate the effect of general caufes. A fcarcity of grain, which no minifterial precautions can altogether remedy; the accumulation of taxes, however judicious in their felection, or indifpenfable; laftly, the neceffity of affixing fome limit to popular meetings and popular declamations, may irritate to refentment, or propel to refiftance.

The command of armies, and the direction of fenates, muft neceffarily be entrufted to the few : but the field of glory and utility is notwithftanding ample and extenfive.

extenfive. Every good man will refift, and
every wife man will oppofe the dangerous
fpirit of innovation, which characterizes
the prefent moment. Thofe who by whatever caufe are precluded from active employment, may yet by their exertions render effential fervice to their common country. An intelligent and beautiful hiftorian
of antiquity, has eftimated the praife of him
who narrates, as only beneath that of him
who acts. " *Vel pace, vel bello, clarum*
" *fieri licet.—Ac mihi quidem, haud qua-*
" *quam par gloria fequatur fcriptorem &*
" *auctorem rerum, tamen in primis arduum*
" *videtur res geftas fcribere.*" The motives which actuated the author of the Cata-
linian confpiracy, equally impel the writer
of the following fheets. Whatever may be
his inferiority in talents and capacity, he
may challenge to equal the Roman hiftorian
in the purity of his views, and in the rectitude of his intentions.

The

The prefent war, of which we univerfally lament the neceffity, which has fo
greatly aggravated all the public burdens,
and which during its progrefs has been diftinguifhed by fuch perpetual viciffitudes of triumph and of defeat, derives its origin and its
juftification from the decrees of the French
democracy. To that fource may be clearly
traced all the calamities which actually de-
folate Europe, and which are felt to the extremities of the globe. If we were called
upon to point out the particular period in the
courfe of the laft and prefent century, when
the condition of the civilized world was
moft tranquil, profperous, and happy, we
fhould probably felect the interval which
elapfed between the fignature of peace with
France in the beginning of 1783, and the
month of July, 1789. The troubles, excited in
the Auftrian Netherlands by the imprudent
and injudicious regulations of the Emperor
Jofeph, and the rapid invafion, or rather
conqueft

conqueft of Holland by the Duke of Brunf-
wick, affected for a time, but did not de-
ftroy, the general ferenity.

It is impoffible not to look back with
mingled pleafure and regret, to this flat-
tering and tranfitory calm which preceded
the tempeft. Never were all the arts that
minifter to elegance, tafte, and refinement,
more affiduoufly or univerfally cultivated.
Navigation explored the moft diftant feas,
and commerce expanded itfelf in every direction. The facilities of communication,
intercourfe, and correfpondence, might be
faid in fome meafure to approximate the ca-
pitals of Europe. A gentler police, and a
more mitigated or liberal jurifprudence, fof-
tened the rigours of arbitrary power, in all
the countries where it exifted. The feverity
of defpotifm began every where to fink under its own weight, or to diffolve in its own
weaknefs. The " privileged orders," as
they

they have fince been invidioufly denomi-
nated, were no longer feparated by infupe-
rable barriers from their fellow citizens.
The nominal elevation derived from birth,
title, and fituation, continued indeed every
where to fubfift; but nothing offenfive adhered to the diftinction.

Every employment was open to talents,
induftry, and merit. A love of letters, and
a paffion for literature, eminently characterized the time, while it diffufed its influence over fociety. The productions of genius were not confined to the apartments of
the great, or the libraries of the ftudious;
but, pervaded every rank of men. Honors
almoft approaching to idolatry, and fcarcely
inferior to thofe affigned by Athens to So-
crates and Plato, were conferred on fuch as
had contributed by their writings to enlighten,
to improve, or to emancipate mankind.
We may reafonably doubt, whether fince

C   the

the reign of Trajan and the Antonines, Europe has ever enjoyed fo much felicity. But it was foon perceived by men of difcernment, that under the mafk of freedom and philofophy, infidelity and licentioufnefs had begun to produce a filent fermentation in the human mind. It is a queftion which pofterity may be called to decide upon the fulleft evidence, whether the extremes of ignorance and of information, like thofe of light and darknefs, are not nearly allied; and whether the diffemination of knowledge beyond a certain point, may not be productive of greater convulfions, than have ever been attributed to the effects of defpotifm and fuperftition.

The era of the French Revolution terminated the repofe of Europe. The conftituent and legiflative affemblies, advancing progreffively through all the gradations of violence, outrage, and crime, were ulti-

4   mately

mately loft and fwallowed up in the National Convention. A name which will
convey to remote pofterity the compendious
idea of every incongruity and atrocity, that
can debafe or difhonour the human fpecies.
Equally the fcourge of France, and of fur-
rounding nations, they form the moft awful
phœnomenon which has ever appeared in
the moral, or political world. It was not
merely the depofition and juridical murder
of an amiable, a virtuous, and an innocent
prince, which abftractedly confidered, and
unconnected with other circumftances,
would either have impelled, or could have
juftified the Englifh miniftry, in declaring
war againft the new Republic. Even the
tribute of forrow which we pay to his me-
mory, is in fome meafure diminifhed, when
we reflect that he neither witneffed the tyranny of Robefpierre, nor the total deftruction of his kingdom. " *Non vidit obfef-*
" *fam curiam, et claufum armis fenatum,*

" *et*

" *et eadem strage tot consularium cædes,*
" *tot nobilissimarum fœminarum exsilia et*
" *fugas.*" His last hours were cheered
by the confolations of religion; and he
carried to the fcaffold the conviction, that
his death, by extinguishing the rage of
faction and the hatred of monarchy, would
reftore univerfal tranquillity. The punifh-
ment of that flagitious act, whatever abhorrence it excites, might have been fecurely
entrufted to the retribution of a juft and
avenging Providence. Nor can it be denied
that the Convention could have found in
our own annals a precedent, which however
diffimilar or deteftable, might neverthelefs
have appeared not totally inapplicable to the
trial and execution of Louis the Sixteenth.

Even the fubfequent aggreffions committed by France; the conqueft of Savoy,
the irruption into Germany, the invafion of
the Auftrian Netherlands, and the avowed
determination of opening the navigation of
the

the Schelde in defiance of treaties : these proceedings, however subversive of the balance of power, and injurious to the interests of Great Britain, might yet have been tolerated by a supine, or perhaps submitted to by a pacific and cautious minister. Only sixty years ago, under the late reign, when Naples and Sicily were wrested from the House of Austria, and a third monarchy, in addition to those of France and Spain, was erected in favour of a prince of the family of Bourbon, England remained a passive spectatress of so important a change. The eventual incorporation of the duchy of Lorrain with the French crown, which was stipulated at the same time, an acquisition of inestimable value, from the extent of its territory, and the protection afforded by it to the vulnerable frontier of Champagne ; yet could not induce Sir Robert Walpole, though a consummate and experienced statesman, to have recourse to arms.

After

After the death of the Emperor Charles the Sixth in 1741, when by order of Louis the Fifteenth, Maillebois, at the head of an army entered Weftphalia, overawed Hanover, and menaced the fubverfion of the Germanic fyftem, the court of St. James's long adhered to temporizing meafures. It was not till after feveral years of ineffectual negotiation, that George the Second joined his forces to thofe of Maria Therefa. In times ftill more recent, fince the exiftence of the prefent adminiftration, when Jofeph the Second violated the barrier treaty, ejected the Dutch garrifons, and demolifhed all the fortreffes in the Low Countries, from the citadel of Antwerp to the gates of Namur, only remonftrances were made by England. Even the infraction of the peace of Weftphalia by the fame prince in opening the Schelde, and his unprovoked hoftilities againft Holland, did not alter the meafures of a miniftry, which has manifefted on

every

every occasion its predilection and attachment to peace.

It may safely be asserted, that the justi-
fication of the present war with France is
not merely deduced from considerations of
policy, but rests upon foundations as broad
and as solid, as the existence and preservation
of civil society itself. The decree of fraternization, adopted by the Convention as
early as the month of November, 1792, and
which was passed by acclamation, amounted
to an unqualified declaration of hostility
against every regular government. It went
further; since it excited to insurrection the
lower classes, promised assistance, on the
part of the republic, to all who wish to procure liberty, and even charged the executive
power " to co-operate, through the me-
" dium of the French generals, with such
" people as have suffered, or are now suf-
" fering in the cause of freedom."

Imagi-

Imagination can scarcely conceive an engine more powerful, or more calculated to subvert every principle of obedience, and to render Europe a theatre of universal rebellion. Correspondent effects resulted from it ; and the impression made by those which took place throughout this island, is too deep and too recent, to need either recapitulation or allusion. Societies, formed upon the model of the Jacobin clubs which had deluged Paris with blood, imbued with similar tenets, and holding a regular intercourse, were established. Productions, capable of seducing, irritating, and inflaming the populace to acts of outrage, were distributed with impunity. The fermentation, excited by these daring acts, was such as to affect public credit, and to spread the utmost consternation mixed with despondency, over the metropolis itself. An administration so infatuated as not to have perceived, so credulous as to have doubted, or so supine as

not

not to have checked the evil in its origin, muft have been equally negligent, criminal, and contemptible. Even the leaft delay would have been fatal and irremediable. With a magnanimity and wifdom adequate to the emergency, they embraced the moft decifive meafures. They affembled the parliament, embodied the militia, ordered the French ambaffador to quit the kingdom, and diffipated in fome meafure, by the energy of their exertions, the gloom which pervaded the nation.

If, in addition to the motives for commencing war, drawn from the internal fituation of Great Britain, any further reafons were wanting to juftify it, they would prefent themfelves on contemplating the picture of Europe, as it exifted at the beginning of 1793. The outline is fo bold, and the features are fo prominent, that they only require to be traced with accuracy and

D   fidelity.

fidelity. The Auſtrian and Pruſſian armies, after having penetrated into the heart of Champagne, and menaced Paris itſelf, had been compelled from a variety of cauſes, the enumeration of which is equally painful and unneceſſary, to evacuate with ignominy the territories of France. Nearly at the ſame period, the Duke of Saxe Teſchen, who had commenced the ſiege, or more properly the bombardment of Liſle, was reduced to abandon the enterprize with ſimilar precipitation. Dumouriez, who has acquired ſuch celebrity, and who occupies ſo diſtinguiſhed a place in the hiſtory of the preſent time, entering Haynault, drove before him the Imperial troops. The memorable battle of Gemappe rendered him maſter of the Netherlands; and diſplayed in the moſt conſpicuous point of view, the imprudent policy of Joſeph the Second, who had diſmantled thoſe expoſed and important provinces. Every city opened its gates, and

Bruſſels

Bruffels fubmitted to the conqueror. The citadels of Antwerp and Namur capitulated, after a feeble refiftance. Luxemburgh alone, of all the places in the Low Countries, continued to acknowledge the Emperor. Purfuing his advantages with incredible celerity, the French commander overtook and defeated Clairfayt, under the walls of Tirlemont. On the following day he entered Liege, where he was received without oppofition. So rapid a train of victories had not been witneffed by Europe, fince the appearance of Guftavus Adolphus in the laft century.

The operations of Cuftine in another quarter, were fcarcely lefs fuccefsful. Having affembled his forces at Landau, he attacked the Auftrians drawn up before Spires, completely routed them, and fucceffively captured that city, Worms, and Mentz. Paffing the Rhine, Francfort furrendered;

and though it was afterwards re-taken, the confternation excited by the French conquefts, fpread into Franconia, the Palatinate, and Heffe. Montefquieu had previoufly achieved with the utmoft facility, the reduction of Savoy ; while another body of troops, croffing the Var, took poffeffion of Nice. The Convention, intoxicated with their good fortune, forgetful of their recent renunciation of foreign conquefts, and yielding to the impulfe of rapacity, or ambition, decreed that Savoy fhould be immediately annexed to France, under the name of " the department of the Mont " Blanc." Such were the firft fruits of the boafted " Rights of Man," and fuch the refpect manifefted for the principles, upon which the republic itfelf was founded !

The afpect of the interior of France prefented at this juncture, an impofing, though

a fala fallacious picture of comparative profperity and ferenity. The maffacres of September had been confined principally to the metropolis. In the Convention, the party of " the Gironde " contended, it is true, for fuperiority with that of " the Moun- " tain:" but their recriminations were in a great degree confined to the walls of the Affembly. No fymptoms of counter revolutionary principles had openly manifefted themfelves at Lyons ; nor had " federa- " lifm" reared its head at Toulon and at Marfeilles. The fermentation in the weftern provinces, had not yet produced the infurrection of La Vendée, in favour of loyalty and religion. Victory accompanied the arms of the republic beyond the frontiers ; while the immenfe confifcations arifing from the royal and ecclefiaftical revenues, feemed to furnifh an inexhauftible fund for fupplying the expences of the war.

Holland,

Holland, torn by two inveterate factions, and deftitute of a military force adequate to its own defence, was menaced with an immediate invafion by Dumouriez. William the Fifth, Stadtholder of the United Provinces, clofely united by ties of the intereft and policy with Great Britain, looked to that crown for protection ; but, though nominally invefted with the dignities, he had not fucceeded to the authority and confideration, poffeffed by the princes of Orange in the laft century. The court of Madrid betrayed in all its conduct a mixture of irrefolution and timidity. Charles the Fourth, who fince his acceffion to the throne of Spain, has difplayed little energy or exertion, had made an ineffectual application, through the medium of his ambaffador at Paris, to avert, or to protract the execution of Louis the Sixteenth. The indignation which he muft neceffarily have felt at the contemptuous rejection of his requeft in favour of

the

the chief of his family, and the numerous
motives, political and perfonal, which ſti-
mulated to revenge his death, appeared
neverthelefs, unequal to impel him to hazard a rupture with ſo formidable a power
as the new republic.

Italy awaited its fate in ſilence and con-
ſternation. The King of Sardinia, de-
ſpoiled of a part of his dominions, limited
his efforts to the preſervation of the remainder, and was ſolely occupied in de-
fending the paſſages of the Alps which open
an entrance into Piedmont. Genoa might
almoſt be conſidered as a dependent pro-
vince of France ; and Ferdinand, great
Duke of Tuſcany, notwithſtanding his
proximity of blood to the head of the empire, ſeemed little inclined to ſacrifice the
trade of Leghorn to the intereſts of his bro-
ther. Pius the Sixth had been early marked
out for the vengeance of the Convention,
irritated

irritated at the protection which he extended to the perfecuted clergy and expatriated nobility, who fought an afylum at Rome. That pacific and opulent city, the antient capital of the world, offered befides, a tempting and a defencelefs object of plunder. The French already facked it by anticipation, and meditated to remove the mafter-pieces of Grecian fculpture, from the palace of the Vatican, to the gallery of the Louvre. The King of the two Sicilies, as a defcendant of the Houfe of Bourbon, was neceffarily involved in the effects of the enmity borne towards every individual of that family. Naples itfelf was overawed by the vicinity of Toulon; and the Neapolitan marine, though fully adequate to the defence of their own coafts againft pirates or Algerines, could not venture to conteft the empire of the Mediterranean with the navy of the republic.

Among

Among the European potentates, who by their local pofition were removed to a diftance from the fcene of action, Guftavus the Third was eminently diftinguifhed. His antient and hereditary connection with the French monarchs, the ardour of his mind, and perhaps a wifh to fignalize his military talents on fo confpicuous a theatre, impelled him to declare war againft the Convention. But neither the refources of Sweden, nor the inclination of his fubjects, feconded his intentions. Denmark embraced a cautious and interefted neutrality. Catherine the Second, protected by the intervention of a vaft portion of Europe, and ftill more by the genius and character of the Mufcovites, from the danger of immediately imbibing the contagion of democracy, manifefted in edicts her abhorrence of the French principles; but abftained from any act of hoftility againft France. Occupied with her projects for the final fubjugation of Poland, and anxioufly attentive to every movement

E of

of the Porte, fhe refufed, or declined to join her forces to thofe of the combined powers. The court of Conftantinople, on the other hand, though that capital had been in every age the favourite feat of defpotifm, yet feduced by the blandifhments, or corrupted by the prefents of the Convention, profeffed fentiments of amity towards the Affembly.

It was in this awful and momentous crifis, when the armies of **Auftria and Pruffia were flying or vanquifhed,** and the other powers of Europe were intimidated from entering into the conteft, that the **Englifh miniftry** met the danger. The decree of hoftilities againft the King of England, iffued by the National Convention on the 1ft of February, 1793, than which nothing could be a more open and direct aggreffion on the part of France, left us, indeed, no choice as to peace or war. The prefervation of Holland was the immediate confequence of our interference. If, deluded by the proteftations, or terrified by the menaces of France, we had permitted

her

her to diffeminate her tenets, while fhe extended her conquefts, the antient order of events was at an end. Great Britain might, perhaps, for a fhort time, have monopolized or enjoyed the commerce of the world: but, its conftitution, laws, and independence were virtually loft. Pofterity will acknowledge the obligation, and will own with gratitude, that to the magnanimous exertions of a fingle nation, may be principally afcribed the duration of regulated freedom, moral order, and religion, throughout the civilized earth.

The conduct of the war in its various branches, opens a widely different fubject of difcuffion, and has afforded to the enemies of adminiftration a copious field of cenfure. The attack upon Dunkirk, the evacuation of Toulon, the expedition to Quiberon, and the operations in the Weft Indies, have all been arraigned or con-

E 2 demned

demned in turn with unqualified afperity. On one point only, no difference of opinion has exifted. The moft difcontented and the moft defponding admit, that at no former period of our hiftory, has the naval fuperiority of Great Britain been fo uniformly maintained, or its glory fo much augmented. The engagement of the 1ft of June, 1794, rivals in fplendor the victory of the 12th of April, 1782, and places the name of Howe at leaft on an equality with that of Rodney. Its effect is heightened, if we reflect on the fpirit of terror, ferocity, and fanaticifm, which animated the French nation under the tyranny of Robefpierre. The action of the 23d of June in the prefent year, fought upon the coaft of the enemy, and at the entrance of their harbours, reflected the higheft honour on the fkill, intrepidity, and talents of the Englifh commander. The fcene had been already immortalized by the defeat of Conflans in 1759,

1759, and recalls to every reader the tro-
phies acquired by Hawke. Even the re-
treat of Cornwallis before a fuperior force,
infpired not lefs admiration and refpect;
than it difplayed the triumph of nautical
ability and deliberate valour.

In the Mediterranean, the national character has acquired additional luftre. Italy has
been protected from invafion, not by her
own exertions, or by the navy of Spain, but
folely by the fleet of George the Third. Corfica has been reduced to the obedience of the
crown, in defiance of the defperate efforts
of a part of the inhabitants, aided by
France. After a war which has lafted
nearly three years, only two fhips of the
Englifh line, the " Cenfeur" and the
" Berwick," have been added to the fleet
of the republic; nor can the French vanity
derive the flighteft gratification from the
circumftances which accompanied their capture. Nearly half the navy of France has
been,

been, within the fame period of time, de-ftroyed or taken; and the remainder is either blocked-up, or compelled to feek re-fuge under the batteries of Breft and of Toulon.

So manifeft has been the weaknefs, and fo avowed the naval inferiority of France during the prefent war, that they have not even ventured to attempt the fyftematical protection of their diftant eftablifhments. In India, Pondicherry has fallen, and the French are expelled from every part of the peninfula. The recent reduction of the Cape of Good Hope has added equal folidity and ftability to the foundations, on which reft the duration and profperity of the Eaft India Company. That fettlement, fituated at the fouthern extremity of Africa, in a falubrious and temperate climate, may from its local pofition, be rendered a military ftation, and a depofit of troops, always

ready

ready to be fent to the aid of our wide extended dominions in Bengal, and on the
two coafts of Coromandel and of Malabar.
The variety of its productions, and pecu-
liarly the quantity of grain which may be
raifed and exported from the Cape, increafe the importance of the acquifition.
Its value to Great Britain would be inefti-
mable, if retained at a treaty of peace.

We have every reafon to fuppofe that at
this time, not only Cochin, but the ifland
of Ceylon is in our poffeffion. Malacca can
make little refiftance. Even Batavia itfelf,
the capital of Java, and the metropolis of all
the Dutch poffeffions in that part of the
world, is incapable of a long, or an effec-
tual defence. Amboyna, from which we
were expelled under James the Firft, may
return to the crown of England; and the
Banda iflands would fall almoft without a
blow. The downfall of that prodigious
empire

empire, and that lucrative .commerce, founded by Holland in .the. sixteenth and seventeenth centuries, on the ruins of the Portuguese greatnefs in Afia, opens a wild field for enterprize, and a striking subject for reflection. It can only be averted by the speedy termination of the war.

After the exhilarating profpect which our affairs in the Eaft present, it is lefs pleasing to direct the view beyond the Atlantic. Yet, even in the Weft Indies, where the efforts of the enemy have been moft vigorous, their operations feem rather directed to devaftation than to conqueft, and more productive of revenge than of victory. In the re-capture of Guadaloupe, they were aided by a concurrence of fortunate circum- ftances, which they unqueftionably .improved by celerity and decifion. The fpirit of. rebellion and infurrection, fomented among the negroes, which has caufed fuch

de-

deplorable ravages and fo vaft an effufion of
blood, has been little aided by the exertions,
or directed by the wifdom of the convention.
In St. Domingo, where we ftill occupy fome
of the moft important pofts, the only infu-
perable obftacles to our progrefs have been
found in the pernicious nature of the climate,
in the difficulty of fubfifting the troops, and
in the impracticability of retaining poffeffions fo widely extended. Martinico may
defy all attack: the other iflands are rather
plundered and defolated by banditti, than
fubjected to France, from which country
they can only draw a precarious affiftance,
and to which they fcarcely own a nominal
fubjection. Victor Hugues, the national
commiffioner, may be more juftly regarded
in the light of a defperate buccaneer, than as
the general of an army acting under the direc-
tions of the Republic. The formidable naval
and military equipment which has recently
failed from Spithead, will probably fix on

perma-

permanent foundations, the fupremacy of England in the weftern hemifphere.

The vigilant and unremitted protection extended to our commerce, is entitled to the higheft commendation, and will appear more meritorious, if contrafted with antecedent periods of Englifh hiftory, which we are accuftomed to confider as profperous. Notwithftanding the brilliant victory of La Hogue, fo celebrated in our annals, the reign of William the Third prefents in every page a melancholy lift of captures, and of depredations effected by the enemy. Whole fleets of merchantmen were intercepted, and the channel fwarmed with French Privateers. The admiral of Louis the Fourteenth anchored in Torbay, burnt the towns on the coaft of Devon, and fpread terror from Beachy Head to the Land's End. Under the fucceeding reign, while Lord Godolphin prefided at the Treafury, and while Marl-

borough

borough triumphed in Flanders, neither the
trade nor the coafts of the kingdom were better protected.

During the long adminiftration of Sir Robert Walpole, though for the greater part pacific, the debates in Parliament, and the com-
plaints of the mercantile part of the nation
fufficiently prove, how feverely we fuffered
from the Spanifh Guarda Coftas, and how
inadequate were the meafures adopted by government for repelling fuch outrages. I need
not recall the humiliating recollection of the
late war, when d'Orvilliers, at the head of
the combined fleets, infulted Plymouth, and
when fcarcely a convoy arrived at its port, or
reached its deftination. If we confider the
immenfe extent of the actual traffic carried
on by England, we fhall perhaps admit that
no precautions can preclude difafter in every
inftance. Yet, with the exception of the late
audacious and fortunate enterprife of Rich-

ery,

ery, executed in defiance of a fuperior fleet cruizing off the harbour of Toulon, we have fcarcely fuftained any capture of magnitude or importance.

If from the confideration of our commer‑ cial, maritime, and colonial interefts, we di‑ rect our view to the military operations on the continent, little apparent fubject offers itfelf for national exultation. The cam‑ paigns of 1793, and of the following year, prefent a feries of difafters, calamities, and de‑ feats, checquered, it is true, by fome tranfient gleams of advantage and fuccefs. After the failure of the attempt upon Dunkirk, every rational hope of penetrating into the interior provinces of France, was at an end. It is, however, generally afferted and believed, that if fubfequent to the furrender of Valen‑ ciennes, the combined armies had inftantly advanced againft Cambray and Bouchain, they might have entered Artois and Picardy,

through

through the breach effected in the barrier. Thofe, neverthelefs, who recollect that Marlborough and Eugene, the fuperiority of whofe talents, and the extent of whofe views no man difputes, were unable in nine campaigns to break through the chain of garrifons erected by Louis the Fourteenth for the protection of his dominions, will, perhaps, hefitate before they lend an implicit faith to fo queftionable an affertion. The unfuccefsful invafion of the Duke of Brunfwic in the preceding autumn, certainly held out no encouragement to the Prince of Cobourg, to repeat a fimilar experiment. In the fubfequent failure of Dumouriez to awaken the loyalty, or to fhake the adherence of his foldiery to the Convention, the allies muft have perceived how precarious was any reliance on the expectation of a counter revolution.

It may be juftly doubted whether the combined armies were ever fufficiently ftrong to
have

have undertaken the ſiege of Liſle. When
Marlborough, after the victory of Oude-
narde, ventured to ſit down before it in
1708, he did not achieve its reduction under four months. Above eighteen thouſand
men periſhed in the trenches, and no part of
the works was carried without a battle. Yet,
we can hardly ſuppoſe that it would have
been leſs obſtinately defended, than when
Boufflers commanded in the place. To have
raiſed the ſiege, muſt have been deſtructive
to all the future enterpriſes of the allies, and
would have covered them with diſhonour.
To have plunged into the country of the
enemy, without previouſly reducing Liſle,
would have expoſed them to every poſſible
hazard or misfortune; and might have re-
newed in Europe the ignominious capitula-
tions of York-town and Saratoga, ſo memorable in the hiſtory of America.

Obſtacles

Obstacles of the most complicated kind, and which were, perhaps, in their own nature insurmountable, opposed the progress of the combined armies. The inveterate animosity, or rather antipathy, which has subsisted during more than half a century, since the conquest of Silesia, between the courts of Berlin and Vienna, was not calculated to produce unanimity between the generals or troops of their respective sovereigns. To the versatile conduct, and to the crooked or interested policy of Frederic William, may be attributed the failure of the best concerted plans of the two campaigns. Holland was no longer animated by the exhortations of William the Third, nor directed by the councils of the pensionary Heinsius. If the Dutch had possessed any portion of the spirit, which impelled them to oppose the tyranny of Philip the Second and the Duke of Alva, Pichegru could never have penetrated into the United Provinces. Nature herself seemed to

conspire

confpire for their deftruction. The rigors of winter in 1795, were not lefs favourable to the arms of the French republic, by freezing the great rivers which cover the frontier, than the extreme heats of fummer in 1672, were to Louis the Fourteenth, in facilitating the paffage of the Rhine. It was not poffible to defend a country, the inhabitants of which had loft every fenfe of glory, and every wifh of independence. Sunk in apathy, or contaminated with principles of democracy, they expelled their protectors, and received the enemy with acclamations.

The united effect of thefe caufes was however, inconfiderable, when compared with the gigantic exertions made by France. We cannot contemplate without a mixture of incredulity and aftonifhment, the decree adopted by the Convention, for compelling the people to rife in a mafs. Though ultimately ruinous in its confequences, we muft,

I

never-

neverthelefs admit, that no act of the Roman Senate in the confular ages, even after the defeats at Thrafymene and at Cannæ, when the republic appeared to be on the point of diffolution, equalled it in magnitude, or furpaffed it in energy. It was found on trial impracticable for any of the antient and regular governments of Europe, however arbitrary, to imitate, or to realize the fame expedient. Neither the tactics, the difcipline, nor the conftancy of the Germans, could refift the impetuous and inceffant attacks of an armed multitude, propelled on one hand by the operation of terror, and perfuaded on the other, that they were combating in the caufe of freedom. Only Robefpierre and his colleagues, who trampled no lefs on the laws of humanity, than they defpifed every confideration deduced from ordinary policy, could have torn from the peaceful occupations of hufbandry and agriculture, the peafantry of

G whole

whole provinces, and have inftantly converted them into foldiers. Only a revolutionary government, attended by inftru-
ments of death, could have directed the
unwieldy ftrength, or prevented the difor-
ders and exceffes of fo ftupendous an engine. Europe might have been overrun by
new hordes of civilized barbarians, who
were fubjected to the feverity of military
laws, and conducted by leaders equally ra-
pacious, enthufiaftic, and defperate.

France itfelf prefented during fourteen
months, from the period of the deftruction
of the Gironde faction, to the fall of Robefpierre, the formidable appearance of a
military democracy, actuated by the ener-
gies, the fecrefy, and the decifion of defpotifm. If that tyranny had continued long
to fubfift in all its force, it is difficult to fay
what limits could have been affixed to its
progrefs, or at what point it might have
ftopped.

stopped. But, happily for mankind, its
sanguinary exceffes difgusted and revolted
the French themselves. The Convention,
terrified at the profcription of a number of
their own members, and holding their existence only by the arbitrary will of a mer-
cilefs dictator, were reduced to the alterna-
tive of crushing him, or becoming the paf-
five slaves of his caprice. They found refources in their own defpair, and in the af-
fections of the people. The death of Robefpierre forms an era in the history of
France, and of mankind. It was followed
by the gradual fuppreffion of the fystem of
terror, which had fo long fuperfeded the
rights of human nature, and by indications
of reviving moderation and religion.

All the acts of the government fince that
period, manifeft a filent, but progreffive re-
vulfion in principles and in opinion. The
deftruction of monarchy, and the profcrip-

tion

tion of kings, no longer forms the avowed object of the war ; nor does France afpire to render modern Europe, · like antient Greece, exclufively republican. Even the impotent denunciations of vengeance, or expreffions of enmity againft England, fo frequently repeated from the tribune, are diminifhed in their afperity. Many of the vifionary, or pernicious tenets, precipitately adopted in the fury of democracy, have been virtually abandoned. The very epithets and names, calculated to increafe the hatred of royalty, fink infenfibly into difufe and oblivion.

In the forms, as well as in the effence of the new conftitution recently promulgated, we trace with fatisfaction a degree of fimilarity to our own. The imaginary equality of man difappears, and property is recognized as the indifpenfable requifite or bafis of government. It is no longer a tumultu-

ous

ous affembly, governed by clubs, furrounded by a clamorous populace, and impelled
or withheld in its deliberations by galleries,
that frames laws by acclamation. We fee
on the contrary, two chambers, which in
their comparative numbers and modes of
conducting public bufinefs, bear no very
diftant refemblance to the two Houfes of
Parliament. The regal dignity and functions, without its title, are committed to
the " executive directory ;" or in more cor-
rect language, the crown is put into com-
miffion. In the " Coftume" affumed by the
members of the legiflative body, we almoft
behold the revival of the extinguifhed infig-
nia of knighthood. Louis the Fourteenth
never gave audience at Verfailles, with more
affectation of pageantry and fplendor, than
the " directory" recently exhibited at the
Palace of the Luxembourg, on the firft pre-
fentation of the foreign ambaffadors. Nor is
this change confined to the capital. In the ar-

mies

mies, where the spirit of Robespierre has sur-
vived, and where the same generals who received their commissions from that usurper,
still continue to command, a softer tone and
more polished manners insensibly predominate. Every thing announces the decline of
anarchy, and the termination of those sanguinary scenes, which have almost obliterated
in atrocity the massacre of St. Bartholomew.

While we revolve in thought the history
of France since the revolution, it is difficult not to direct our eye forwards to its future destiny, and not to ask in what form or
mode of government the nation will finally
acquiesce. Never, perhaps, was a wider
subject opened for conjecture; and never
did any derive less assistance from the ordinary sources of light. Reason, policy,
and experience, the only guides, cannot
enable us to pronounce even with probabi-
lity. Yet we may incline to believe, on the

most

most mature confideration, that if the republic continues " one and indivifible," it muft
ultimately fix in limited monarchy. Seven
years have not yet paffed fince July 1789,
and fcarcely three fince the execution of
Louis the Sixteenth. We may recollect that
eighteen years intervened between the commencement of the great rebellion in this
country, and the reftoration of monarchy.
Above eleven elapfed from the death of
Charles the Firft, to the recall of his fon.
Louis the Eighteenth at Verona, is certainly
not more forgotten, than was Charles the
Second at Cologne ; nor has France, like
England under Cromwell, paffed into the
permanent dominion of another family. If
the prefent century fhould not fee the crown
reftored to the Houfe of Bourbon, it will
probably take place at no remote period of
the enfuing one. The war actually waged
againft France, has unqueftionably not ac-
celerated fo defirable an event. As well
might

might Henry the Sixth be re-proclaimed, as a king be impofed upon the nation by force. Time, peace, and the infenfible operation of many emotions, fufpended or extinguifhed during a period of civil difcord, can alone rebuild the throne, or place it on folid foundations.

The actual fituation of France, notwithftanding the advantages fhe had obtained on the continent, and the extent of territory which fhe ftill continues to occupy, is yet, if accurately examined, little calculated to infpire alarm or apprehenfion. That fpirit of ferocious enthufiafm, fuftained and propelled by terror, which characterifed the infancy of the republic, and which in its firft energy threatened to fubvert every government throughout Europe, is already far advanced in its decline. The bulwarks, oppofed to its progrefs, and the intervention of two campaigns, however unfortunate on

the

the fide of the allies, have checked the French impetuofity, and allowed the firft paroxyfm of national frenzy to fubfide. The people, exhaufted by efforts above their ftrength, long humbled under a tyranny not lefs ignominious than fanguinary, and convinced of the inanity or impracticability of realizing their dreams of equality, feem ardently to demand repofe. They find, that like Ixion, they have miftaken a cloud for a divinity, and behind the ftatue of liberty, have met the axe of the guillotine.

Even in the armies, victory is no longer " permanent," nor conqueft progreffive. The military inundation feems to have attained its utmoft height in the fpring of the prefent year, after the total evacuation of Holland by the allies, when the republican forces occupied all the countries from the heart of Navarre and Catalonia, to the courfe of the Ems, the Waal, and the We-

H   fer.

fer. They have been for the most part, quiescent and stationary during the summer. Peace has withdrawn them from Spain; and in Piedmont, if we except the recent advantage at Vado, their success has been only negative. On the side of the Palatinate, the military operations are again transferred from the banks of the Neckar and the Rhine, to the vicinity of the Moselle. An army has surrendered prisoners of war in Manheim; and the importance of that capture is eloquently, as well as forcibly expressed, in the silence of the French government upon so material an event. The Netherlands are held by a precarious tenure, and may be lost with the same rapidity that they were subjected. Symptoms of discontent and insurrection appear in Holland, where the party of the House of Orange, crushed, but not extinguished, will revive on the first favourable occasion. The genius of the French soldiery has been in every age ill adapted to de-

4   fensive

fenfive war; and their generals, inftead of penetrating into the empire, may now efteem themfelves fortunate, if they can retain their pofts along the river Nahe, or preferve their acquifitions in Belgium. The unfuccefsful attack upon the Auftrian magazines at Heidelberg was the point that decided the fate of Germany, and has been the prelude to greater viciffitudes.

If fuch is the doubtful complexion of the affairs of the Republic beyond the frontiers, its internal condition may be defcribed in ftronger language. All the evils neceffarily refulting from a feries of violence, profcription, and confifcation, are there to be found in their utmoft magnitude. It is not merely the fubverfion of the monarchy, the deftruction of the upper or middle orders, and the indifcriminate plunder of the opulent, which has diftinguifhed the revolution. The people, in whofe name, and for whofe benefit thefe enormities were committed, have been ultimately

its

its greatest victims. Their pretended sovereignty has terminated in famine, and in the most degrading slavery. The finances, oppressed beneath the load of endless millions of assignats perpetually added to the circulation, have, by the confession of their own ministers, attained the point, when any further emission of paper is become destructive of its object. So enormous is the depreciation, that an assignat of the nominal value of one livre, or ten pence halfpenny English, was recently not worth a denier; in other words, the third part of a farthing. Even this statement is below the fact; but, in such a calculation, and amidst such fluctuations, the difference is hardly worth noting. To affix something like value to the mass, or to substitute any other medium of exchange in its place, peace and public confidence are indispensable.

Of the many valuable colonies which she heretofore possessed, only Cayenne on the continent of South America, the islands of

Mauritius

Mauritius in the Indian ocean, and the forts
or factories on the African coaft, continue
fubject to France. The precious metals
have in a great degree difappeared in tranfactions of bufinefs, and are either concealed
by the poffeffors, or have found their way
out of the Republic. It is difficult to conceive a fituation fo deplorable as that defcribed by the minifter of finance, in his recent report to the executive directory, on the
ftate of the treafury. Even a compulfory
loan, enforced by the operation of terror,
and paid in fpecie, if it can prolong the
means of refiftance, can only do fo for
a fhort time. France is no longer able to
draw to herfelf the gold of foreign nations
by her manufactures and her fifheries, or
even to fupply her own preffing wants.
Neither the defpotifm of the government,
nor the energy of the people, can remedy
thefe accumulated misfortunes, though their
effect may be palliated, or the term of na-

tional

tional bankruptcy may poffibly be protracted by a variety of expedients.

Paris itfelf, notwithftanding fome external and fallacious indications of fplendor, pleafure, or diffipation, prefents only the emaciated figure of its former opulence. Almoft all the trades and profeffions, that require manual delicacy, or which depend on tafte and invention, have become extinct. Gold, filver, and fteel, metals excluſively appropriated to the more elegant branches of workmanfhip, can no longer be employed, from a want of artifts. The fame hands which formerly organized the mechanifm of a watch, or gave its laft exquifite polifh to the fciffars, have been directed to the operation of cafting artillery, and roughened in forging pikes or mufquets. A new race of artificers is wanting, as well as new materials. The tapeftry of the Gobelins, with which the palaces of princes were decorated,
remains

remains unfinifhed in the looms; and the
fuperb porcelain of Seve has been long no
more.

In the provinces, depopulation and mifery
are equally vifible, and lefs concealed than in
the capital. The flagitious exceffes, committed by the revolutionary commanders in
La Vendée, are not to be perufed without
horror, and have reduced to a defert the
moft fertile portions of France. From the
banks of the Loire to thofe of the Charente,
civil war has defolated all the intermediate
country. Lyons, which in 1789, fed,
while it enriched an immenfe multitude of
induftrious inhabitants, prefents only a heap
of ruins, and a monument of national vengeance. The beautiful fabricks of filk,
which fupplied not only France, but, half
Europe with articles of drefs and ornament,
have been demolifhed. It is only in the deliberate maffacre of the Alexandrians by
Caracalla,

Caracalla, that we can find any parallel in antiquity, to the military executions committed by Collot d'Herbois at Lyons. " *Nero tamen fubtraxit oculos, juffitque fcelera, non fpectavit.*" The French comedian, more inexorable than the worft of the Cæfars, affifted in perfon, and fuperintended the carnage of his fellow citizens " in a mafs." The trade of the Levant no longer fuftains Marfeilles; and Toulon has not yet recovered its naval loffes, or re-conftructed its docks and arfenals. Nantes, from whence fo extenfive a commerce was carried on to the Weft Indies, and beyond the Atlantic, has been the theatre of Carrier's enormities; and during the laft three years, may be faid to have fuffered almoft every calamity incident to a city befieged by foreign enemies. Angers is in a fimilar fituation. At Rouen, the people want not only employment, but fuftenance. The fabrication of the finer fpecies of cloth manufactured at Louviers

and

and at Abbeville, has been in a great meafure fufpended, and only a coarfer kind is
made for general ufe. Even Bourdeaux,
though it feems to have hitheito efcaped the
laft horrors of anarchy or of violence, yet
is fallen into a deplorable ftate of wietched-
nefs. France prefents the image of a vaft
volcano, furrounded with heaps of lava, on
whofe furface, during many years, fcarcely
any trace of verdure will appear.

Notwithftanding this gloomy picture, the
colours of which are far from being over-
charged, we muft not lightly conclude that
the Republic is altogether deftitute of temporary means to continue the war. Even in
meafures pregnant with inevitable future deftruction, fhe may poffibly find a degree of
prefent fafety or relief. The defpotifm of the
government, and the fubmiffion of the people, feem to have neither any acknowledged,
nor any defined limit. We have feen an example of the former, in the decree exacting
within three days a fupply of corn, adequate

I   to

to the confumption of the metropolis during
twelve weeks. The extent of the latter, as
well as the ability of the people to furnifh
the quota required, are matters not lefs cu-
rious in their nature, than important in their
refult. A country, in which the phyfical
properties, or productions of the foil are
compelled at any moment into requifition,
where agriculture is not altogether extinct,
and where the quantity of grain allowed to
every individual, is fuperintended or limited,
may in fome meafure appear to retain tranfitory refources. The revolutionary fpirit,
which has produced fuch ftupendous effects,
though on its decline, has not yet expired.
It may revive under the walls of Landau or
Thionville, if the Auftrians, elated by their
recent and fplendid victories, fhould purfue
the flying army of the republic, and re-
enter Alface, or penetrate again into Champagne. Thofe who affect to poffefs the
moft authentic fources of information, affert that even gold and filver, however at
prefent concealed, are not totally wanting;
and

and that they may in fome degree be found, whenever the exigencies of State force their re-appearance. The contribution of fix hundred millions of livres recently ordered, and which is to be paid principally in fpe-cie, will put this affertion to the teft. Whatever may be the iffue of that loan, the attempt is unexampled, and fufficiently evinces the defperation of the men who have recurred to the meafure.

It cannot, however, be denied, while we contemplate the difaftrous condition of the French Republic, that Great Britain ftands in need of repofe. Her population has been neceffarily diminifhed by three fevere and deftructive campaigns. Whole regiments have fallen victims to the pernicious climate of St. Domingo, or to the maladies of the Weft India iflands. That meritorious clafs of men, who form equally our pride and our protection, the Englifh failors, have

I 2   fuffered

suffered from famine and disease, added to captivity, in the prisons of the republic. Even in the recent misfortune occasioned by adverse winds, which delayed the expedition destined for the West Indies, and in the storms that covered the coast with wrecks, we find matter of private sympathy, and of public regret. The addition of near sixty or seventy millions to the national debt, and the proportional increase of taxes, have been accompanied with a rapid rise in the price of certain branches of workmanship, as well as on many articles of domestic use, or of foreign importation.

These disasters, inseparable from the nature of war, are more severely felt throughout the course of the present hostilities, from the operation of an incidental calamity, the scarcity of corn. It is now pretty well ascertained, that though there has been for many years past, a redundancy of bailey

3   throughout

throughout the kingdom, the quantity of wheat produced has been inadequate to the demand. There is reafon to believe that the evil originates principally from two caufes; an augmented population on one hand, and on the other, an increafed confumption of the finer fpecies of flour, the natural effect of opulence or of luxury. Adventitious circumftances have aggravated, but do not occafion the preffure of which we complain. The troubles and devaftation of Poland, no way to be attributed to the policy of this country; the failure of the harvefts in the provinces along the Lower Danube; the ravages committed by the Republican and Auftrian armies, from the gates of Nimeguen to the borders of Switzerland; the immenfe expenditure of every kind of grain, and the deftruction of magazines during the laft three years; thefe political or phyfical misfortunes, however lefs felt in England than in any other

European

European State, muft yet be confidered as more remote and fecondary caufes of fcarcity. No efforts have been omitted on the part of Adminiftration, to procure fupplies of corn from every part of the world. We may even venture to affert, that in their laudable folicitude to preclude famine, they have fometimes exceeded the dictates of · ordinary policy, and in various inftances gone near to infringe the rights of neutral nations. It has, neverthelefs, been found impoffible altogether to remedy the evil. More favourable feafons, aided by the enlightened and fyftematical attention which the legiflature has now directed to this object, will, we truft, foon enable Great Britain to produce grain adequate to the wants of its inhabitants.

In the fpirit of democracy, or to fpeak more properly, of outrage and fubverfion, by which the prefent times are characterized,

Minifters

Minifters have found a ftill more urgent
and preffing fubject for perpetual circum-
fpection, vigilance, and exertion. The inferior claffes, from obvious caufes, are evi-
dently more fufceptible of pernicious impreffions or exhortations, than at any preceding period. Emiffaries of France, and
profelytes of republicanifm, availing themfelves of thefe circumftances, have found it
no difficult attempt, to miflead their judg-
ments by artful fophiftries, while their paf-
fions are inflamed by malignant mifrepre-
fentations. Affemblies, compofed for the
greater part, of the loweft populace, in dif-
regard of all police, have met to agitate pro-
pofitions, or to difcufs fubjects of the moft
alarming nature. Even the forms of peti-
tion or remonftrance, through which they
may affect to approach the legiflature, only
render the meditated attack more infidi-
ous, by concealing the weapon.

Political

Political theatres and academies have been opened with impunity in various parts of the metropolis, where fedition has been taught as a fcience, and infurrection inculcated as a duty. The artifan, and the mechanic, after the labour or occupation of the day, has been invited by public advertifement, to repair to thefe feminaries of rebellion, and admitted for a fmall pecuniary confideration. Abftract principles of government, and all the " Rights of Man," are there fubjected to his revifion. His imagination is heated, and his reafon perverted, by glowing defcriptions of Utopian purity and perfection, contrafted with an exaggerated picture of the abufes under which he lives. Artful declamation, and pathetic oratory beguile the hour, and infenfibly tranf- form the fober tradefman or the induftri- ous labourer, into a reformer and a poli- tician. He is taught to defpife the inftitu- tions venerated by his anceftors, and to fpurn the reftraints from which freedom

and

and property derive their beft protection. His poverty is infulted by mifreprefented lifts of finecures, penfions, and places, from which he derives no benefit, and towards the payment of which he is informed that he contributes. The conduct of adminiftration, and the misfortunes unavoidably incident to war, offer a copious fource of animadverfion; and minifters are either ridiculed with ftrokes of malicious raillery, or vilified with open invective. To the two Houfes of Parliament he is affured that he cannot look for redrefs, fince they are interefted in perpetuating his grievances, and may not unaptly be compared to the Roman fenate under the worft emperors, in venality, fubferviency, and proftitution. Even the laws and the conftitution themfelves are reprefented as Gothic eftablifhments, demanding a radical reform, obfolete, difproportioned, and unworthy of an enlightened or philofophic people.

K   In

In aid of difcourfe and declamation, the various powers of compofition are invoked. Pamphlets and publications of a thoufand kinds, adapted to the meaneft comprehenfions, fold at the loweft prices, or diftributed gratuitoufly, infinuate their fubtle poifon through the croud. They fharpen the calls of hunger in the neceffitous, direct the attention of the induftrious to fuppofed grievances, and awaken in credulous or timid minds the feeds of difcontent. Every part of the ifland is inundated with thefe productions; and every ftage coach may be made a vehicle to excite diftant counties to infurrection. Poetry is rendered fubfervient to their operation; and the mufe which has been fo long accufed of proftituting to kings her lyre, enlifts under the banners of democracy. Ballads, patriotic fongs, and caricatures, fometimes enlivened by wit, and at others envenomed by fatire, tend to fill up the meafure of difaffection, and to undermine infenfibly the natural attachment of Englifhmen towards their fovereign and their conftitution.

Under fuch circumftances, it might have been fuppofed that a meafure, the fole and unqueftionable object of which was to impofe fome reftriction on popular affemblies and popular harangues, would have met with almoft univerfal approbation and fupport. It muft, neverthelefs, be acknowledged, that fince the memorable Eaft India bill of 1783, none which we have witneffed, has excited more violent debates in both Houfes of Parliament, or produced more clamour throughout the kingdom, than the one for fuppreffing feditious meetings. No arts have been omitted to inflame the populace on fo interefting a point; and with this view, the people have been every where invited to meet, or, in republican language, the " primary affemblies are convened."

K 2   A prin-

A principal leader of the oppofition af-
ferts, that the liberties of the people are virtually extinct, as foon as the bill fhall have
paffed into a law ; and that he has now only
to retire from the ftruggles of public life, to
the private enjoyments of focial friendfhip,
or conviviality. He has even ventured to juftify, if not to inculcate bolder fteps, by declaring that " refiftance to fuch oppreffion,
" is not a queftion of right, but fimply of
" prudence." It is hardly poffible more une-
quivocally to imply and to defcribe the act,
which he feems unwilling or reluctant to
name. The franknefs of the avowal may,
however, be faid to afford fome fecurity
againft the danger of the principle; and an
adminiftration warned, is already prepared
for attack. In the Houfe of Commons, one
of his friends has defcribed by anticipation,
the ftate of abject flavery into which we are
about to fink, and has drawn a comparifon
between the Englifh nation under George
the

the Third, and the Syracufans under the tyranny of the elder Dionyfius. Thefe declamations have neverthelefs failed of their effect; and the tranfitory ferment excited in
the country, is finking faft, as the provifions
of the bill are better underftood, its expe-
diency more clearly afcertained, and its operation more coolly examined.

It would be nugatory in the prefent work
to difcufs the merits of a measure, which
has been fo frequently agitated, and fo mi-
nutely inveftigated by men of the firft talents and capacity. That it is an evil, thofe
who moft applaud and fupport it, may perhaps admit. That it is difficult to regulate
the limits of popular meetings and difcourfes,
without in fome degree diminifhing the right
of affembling and haranguing the people,
cannot be difputed. But, new fituations or
difeafes call for new remedies and exertions.
It is not a confpiracy, or an infurrection in
favour

favour of an exiled prince, that we defire to avert and to reprefs : nor is it a plot, exclufively aimed at the life of the Sovereign, that we alone apprehend. We are not maintaining a parliamentary title againft an hereditary claim ; or fupporting the caufe of limited monarchy· and the proteftant faith, againft popery and ·arbitrary power. For the former of thefe, our anceftors contended, and againft the latter they provided by wife regulations. Our talk is far more arduous, and demands proportionably greater energy or precaution. The example of the French revolution, and the contagion of democracy have fhaken the bafis of civil order itfelf, threatened the fubverfion of every regular government, and involved Europe in univerfal war. Thofe who have witneffed the progreffive advances of licentioufnefs and of fedition among the inferior claffes, during the laft three years, will not regret that for a fimilar period of profpec-

tive

tive time, fome legal reftraint is impofed on their audacity or exceffes.

If any ftronger reafons were wanting to juftify the meafures adopted, they would be found in the recent attack made upon the King himfelf, at the opening of the prefent feffion. Its atrocity is heightened, when we reflect that he was then occupied in one of the moft auguft and folemn functions, infeparably connected with the genius of a free conftitution. Exclufive of the affectionate reverence borne towards the perfon of his Majefty, never, perhaps, was any people fo deeply interefted in the prefervation of a fovereign. His life may be faid not only to guarantee in fome meafure the tranquillity and profperity of his own fubjects: It is connected with the general welfare of Europe, of mankind, and of the world. Scarcely do we dare to anticipate in thought the poffible or probable confequences of his demife,

demife, even at a future and a diftant period.
Still lefs can we contemplate without fhud-
dering, the effects which might have re-
fulted, if in a moment of popular violence
any facrilegious hand had attempted to
abridge the courfe of his life. We rely,
indeed, with full confidence, that under his
fucceffor, the empire will be progreffively
glorious and flourifhing; but thofe who
are moft warmly attached to that illuftrious
perfon, and who anticipate the difplay of his
future virtues, yet truft with loyal folicitude, that the inftant of his acceffion may
be ftill remote.

The reign of George the Third, it is true,
has been marked in its courfe by ftrange
reverfes, by awful viciffitudes, and by vaft
revolutions. He has feen the Englifh
channel in the poffeffion of hoftile fleets;
and the metropolis abandoned to the exceffes of a furious populace, or expofed to
the

the horrors of pillage and conflagration. He has beheld an empire beyond the Atlantic diffevered from his fceptre; nor can it be denied, that during the calamitous period of the American war, his popularity fuffered a temporary diminution, amidft the errors of adminiftration, and the misfortunes of the ftate. Time alone might have effaced thefe impreffions; but they have been more effectually obliterated by the wifdom of his councils, by the beneficence of his government, and by the energy of his fubjects. If the Britifh dominions have been curtailed in America, they are proportionably augmented in Afia. The extenfive and opulent provinces, originally fubjected by the valour of Clive, have been not only preferved, but improved, ameliorated, and rendered at once profperous, and productive of an immenfe revenue. Never, at any period of the prefent reign, were the refources of England fo numerous, or her name fo refpected in every part of the globe, as at this moment.

Venerating

Venerating that conſtitution of which he
is the firſt magiſtrate and the hereditary
guardian, George the Third has never
fought to enlarge the limits of his legitimate
authority; and he has been the faithful
depoſitary of the power entruſted to him by
a great, a free, and a loyal people. They
have repaid his virtues by the nobleſt and
rareſt tribute offered to kings; the only one
which no deſpotiſm can extort, no treaſures
can purchaſe, and no adulation can beſtow:
the tribute voluntarily conferred by mankind on Antoninus Pius, and on Marcus
Aurelius, in antiquity; univerſal homage,
reſpect, and affection. The foundations of
his throne are neither ſuſtained by force,
nor cemented by terror: they reſt on a
firmer baſis, the attachment of his ſubjects.

From the contemplation of the ſovereign,
by an obvious tranſition, we naturally turn
to the perſon in whoſe hands he has veſted
the principal adminiſtration of affairs. Mr.
Pitt is not to be confidered only as the mi-
niſter of the Engliſh Crown: from the pe-
culiar

culiar courfe of events, he is become the central point of Europe. That vaft combination of political governments has looked to him for ftability, at a crifis when they were menaced with diffolution. A fituation, at once fo arduous and fo elevated, has, perhaps, never been attained or occupied by any individual, in the annals of the modern world. If it were not too poetical, we might fay that his panegyric has been made by his enemies, and that his beft eulogium is to be found in the accufations of Briffot, or in the invectives of Barrere. Even in the moment of their greateft triumph or exultation, the French convention feems never to have loft fight of him for a fingle day. Through the medium of their harangues, he appears like fome fuperior being, whofe malignant influence pervaded their councils, overturned their machinations, and fcattered confufion through every department of the republic. Among his

own

own countrymen, where he is viewed with
fcrutinizing eyes, we cannot wonder if his
actions and adminiftration are arraigned
with malevolent ability, or placed in the
moft invidious point of view. -The conduct, the duration, and the reverfes of the
prefent war, have furnifhed to his opponents
copious fubject for animadverfion. Unable
to difpute his talents for peace, his elo-
quence in debate, his fkill in finance, and
his unblemifhed integrity, they infinuate
that he is not equal to directing the complicated machine of ftate, in a time of hoftility or danger. Even his friends and ad-
mirers may, perhaps, reluctantly admit,
that neither his reputation nor his popularity have been able to fuftain without injury,
fo long, and fo rude a trial.

Thofe, neverthelefs, who are accuftomed
to appreciate the characters of public men,
not merely from the event, but by the fituations

tions in which they have acted, or by the obstacles which they have surmounted, will readily allow, that in the course of the last three years, he has displayed equal magnanimity, constancy, and capacity. Placed between the stupendous exertions of France on one hand, and the no less alarming progress of popular ferment on the other, he cannot be tried by former precedents, nor is he amenable to ordinary rules. His predecessors, Lord Godolphin, Sir Robert Walpole, and the Earl of Chatham, opposed only the spirit of ambition, of policy, or of aggrandizement. They resisted kings and regular governments, acting on views and principles, which, however unjust or destructive, were yet recognized. Mr. Pitt has been compelled to struggle with an enemy of a new description, and whose efforts have been directed less to conquest than to extermination. Not to have been overborne in such a contest, is sufficient victory. To have

com-

combated at the head of Europe, in defence
of order and morals ; to have preserved in-
violate our conftitution, our laws, our freedom, and our religion ; thefe negative fuc-
ceffes are equivalent to triumph, and will
not be too dearly purchafed by the greateft
expenditure of national treafure. If his
cotemporaries could difpute his pre-eminent
powers for filling the high ftation he holds,
he might fafely throw himfelf on the juf-
tice of pofterity.

It is unqueftionably the nobleft privilege
of a free conftitution, to difcufs with jea-
lous and vigilant attention every meafure,
the object of which may even indirectly or
eventually diminifh the liberties of the
people. But our regret is only exceeded
by our indignation, when we behold the
inftrument defigned for the prefervation of
freedom, converted into the engine of its
deftruction. The prefent oppofition, if

con-

confidered as a political party, diminifhed as
they are in numbers, and deprived of a great
portion of the property which gave them
weight, are neverthelefs formidable from
the talents of their leaders. Nor will the
merit of induftry, perfeverance, and intrepidity be denied them even by their opponents. It would be infulting the difcernment of fuch a body, to fuppofe that they
did not perceive the fpirit of innovation
which characterizes the prefent age, and
which pervades the lower claffes. It would
impeach the rectitude of their intentions,
to imagine, that perceiving it, they profeffed
to approve of expedients, which ought not
to be even named without the laft neceffity,
and which never can be juftified, except
when ufed againft tyranny. If thefc were
the principles for which Sydney fought,
they certainly were not thofe which Locke
defended, and for which Ruffel bled. As
little were they the political tenets of that
party,

party, diſtinguiſhed in the laſt and preſent century by the name of Whigs; and among which, in times the moſt pregnant with danger, under James the Second, we ſee the conſpicuous names of Cavendiſh, of Wharton, and of Mordaunt. The authors of the revolution which expelled the Houſe of Stuart, and ſeated the family of Brunſwick on the throne, were the friends of regulated freedom, and not the advocates of popular violence and licentiouſneſs. They would have equally reprobated a Thelwall and a Sacheverell; the agents of ſedition, and the defenders or preachers of arbitrary power.

Acroſs the gloom which has covered Europe for ſeveral years, indications of returning tranquillity begin to be viſible. The meſſage recently delivered from the crown to the two Houſes of Parliament, acknowledging the French government as capable of maintaining the accuſtomed relations of

peace

peace and amity, announces its approach. However dubious or remote, the profpect diffufes univerfal fatisfaction. To hazard even a conjecture relative to the time when fo defirable an event may probably take place, or to reafon on the articles which may form the bafis of pacification between the two nations, would be prefumptuous and improper. The tranfactions of war may greatly accelerate or retard its accomplifhment, and muft neceffarily have an influence on the terms ultimately demanded or conceded.

I am arrived at that point, where the nature and limits of the prefent production compel me to ftop. The external fituation of Great Britain at this moment is unqueftionably fuch, as to juftify well-founded expectations of attaining an honorable and advantageous peace, whenever negotiations fhall be commenced. Whatever juft caufe we may have for national folicitude at home, the afpect abroad may bear comparifon with the moft glorious epocha of the Englifh annals,

M   that

that which immediately preceded the treaty of Paris in 1763. We had then, it is true, got poffeffion of Canada, of Martinico, of Gau-daloupe, of Bellifle, of the Havana, of Pon-dicherry, and of Manilla. But, on the other hand, Minorca was fubjected to France. We now hold the keys of both the Indies, and are mafters of Corfica, a far more im-portant and extenfive ifland than Minorca, not merely by conqueft, but from the vo-luntary fubmiffion of the inhabitants. The Cape of Good Hope and Pondicherry, to which we have the happinefs to add the re-cent and important acquifition of Trinco-malé, guarantee the fecurity of our domini-ons in the eaft. Cape Nicola Mole and Mar-tinico open to us the fame profpect in the weft. A country poffeffed of fuch pledges, will not lightly permit the French to retain the Auftrian Netherlands, and to continue virtually mafters of Holland. They will not be induced without the moft cogent rea-fons of State, to allow France to extend her maritime acquifitions from the gates of Dunkirk to thofe of Embden, and to join

3   the

the naval ſtrength of the United Provinces to her own marine. They will not view with indifference the addition of Savoy to her territories, at the expence of a faithful and valuable ally; or the progreſs of the French arms in the county of Nice, and along the coaſt of the Mediterranean. As little will they incline to acquieſce in her making the Rhine the eaſtern boundary of the Republic: a conceſſion which would ſacrifice the independence of Germany, ſubject the empire to new invaſions, and at once overturn the balance of Europe.

Whatever conqueſts the Engliſh nation may be diſpoſed to cede in the Mediterranean, in the Eaſt Indies, or beyond the Atlantic, in order to accompliſh ſo deſirable an object, they will never ſubmit to hold their liberties and their exiſtence at the will of a perfidious, and an ambitious neighbour. Nor will they, from a ruinous and precipi-

tate

tate anxiety to enjoy the advantages of peace, let flip the favourable occafion of rendering it permanent. They will not give to a finking and nearly exhaufted antagonift, a refpite of which fhe will avail herfelf to recruit her forces, and to renew the ftruggle. Exulting in the fuccefs of their paft efforts, they will meet with fortitude the trials which Providence may yet referve for their courage, their conftancy, and their patience. Contending, not as their anceftors did under the Tudors and the Stuarts, for objects of policy, of dominion, or of commerce; but, engaged in the caufe of focial order, of rational freedom, and of every thing that can conftitute the felicity of man in a civilized State, they will continue their exertions, if neceffary, till thefe objects are fecured or accomplifhed.

If we furvey the ftate of Europe at the clofe of 1795, it prefents a diverfified fcene,

in

in which triumph and misfortune, good and ill fuccefs, alternately predominate. The Auftrian Netherlands ftill remain in the hands of the French, and the poffeffion of Luxemburgh feems in fome meafure to cover the eaftern frontier againft invafion. Holland, united with them by recent treaties, and ftill governed by a democratic faction fubfervient to the French Republic, is compelled to abide the termination of the conteft. Deftitute of naval, or military ftrength, crippled in their commerce, bereaved of their moft valuable colonies, and having furvived their political independence, the Dutch can fcarcely be any longer confidered as one of the European States. We may reafonably doubt, whether any thing can again reftore them to the rank and confideration, which they long enjoyed among the maritime powers. If that renovation is ever effected, it can only be produced by a return to their former connections and prin-

4   ciples.

ciples. Pruffia, from unworthy and inex-
plicable motives, has quitted her allies at the
moft critical period of the war : while
Spain, after beholding the republican armies
ready to enter Arragon, and mafters of Bif-
cay, has purchafed a precarious peace, or
more properly a fufpenfion of arms, by the
facrifice of one of her colonies, and with
the diminution of her national honor.

Great as are thefe defalcations and mif-
fortunes, they are fully balanced by corre-
fponding advantages, or new acquifitions.
Francis the Second has difdained to imitate
the treacherous or verfatile policy of Frederic
William. The court of Vienna remains
firm to its engagements ; and fupported by
pecuniary affiftance from Great Britain, the
imperial commanders have made the moft
fuccefsful exertions to drive the enemy from
their pofts upon the Rhine. In Italy, the
Auftrian and Sardinian forces, though recently

cently defeated, continue to defend the paſſages of the Milaneſe and of Piedmont.
Neither Naples, nor Portugal have followed
the example of the cabinet of Madrid.
Catharine the Second is no longer a neutral
ſpectatreſs of the quarrel, and a Ruſſian
ſquadron' acts in conjuction with the fleet
of England.

If the Republic has been on the whole
victorious by land, ſhe is humbled and van-
quiſhed on the ſea. Near ſeven years of
agitation or revolution, and more than three
of civil and foreign war, have exhauſted
the immenſe reſources of the French monarchy. The Metropolis depends for ſub-
ſiſtence on forced requiſitions of grain.
Throughout the provinces, penury and ra-
pine have combined to reduce the wretched
inhabitants to extremity. Manufactures
are at a ſtand, and commerce is extinct.
The moſt ſevere or violent expedients are
adopted,

adopted, in order to raife fupplies of money.
Defeats and defertions have greatly dimi-
niſhed the armies, which under Pichegru
and Jourdan, fo lately threatened to take up
their winter quarters beyond the Rhine.
Numerous levies, and immenfe exertions of
every kind muſt be neceſſary,-to protect the
Netherlands againſt Clairfayt. The French
people, after the depoſition and murder of
their fovereign, the exile or profcription of
their nobility, and the baniſhment or deliberate maſſacre of their clergy, have fallen
a prey to various tyrants and factions.
Wearied with endlefs revolutions, and convinced by experience, that all are alike fanguinary or ruinous, they may be faid to have
at length emerged into fomething like government, and to have formed a conſtitution.

England, though ſhe feverely feels the
misfortunes inferaiable from war, yet has
difplayed invincible fortitude, and refources
of

of every kind, adequate to the magnitude
of the emergency. In the midſt of hoſ-
tilities, her commerce is protected, her
revenue and manufactures flouriſh, and her
credit is unſhaken. The energy of the adminiſtration ſecures the internal tranquillity of
the capital and of the iſland. If their exertions cannot diffuſe plenty, at a moment
when Europe labours under the general want
of grain, we have at leaſt the conſolation of
knowing, that ſcarcity is leſs proportionably
felt than in any other country. The war
had its origin in neceſſity. To the conduct, and the conſequences of it, we may
look with triumph. Whether it terminates
in a few weeks, or whether it ſhould ſtill be
protracted, the great end and object is alike
attained. France has virtually retracted her
principles, has tacitly renounced her tenets,
and has abandoned her pernicious decrees of
fraternization. Whether the Houſe of Bōur-
bon continue to wander in exile, or whe-

N   ther

ther they fhall be recalled to reign again in France, is a confideration of material, but to us of fecondary importance. The form of the French government is not the fubject for which we contend. We are not engaged in the quarrel of a family, or combating in the caufe of monarchy. England has re- luctantly drawn her fword in the defence of her freedom, her conftitution, and her ex- iftence. To her magnanimous perfeverance, Europe has hitherto been indebted for pre- fervation againft the torrent of democracy, immorality, and anarchy. Satisfied with a teftimony fo glorious, we look forward with confidence ; and firmly await the final iffue of the moft awful conteft, in which Britain was ever engaged at any period of her hiftory.

London,
9th January, 1796.

F I N I S.

9 780483 149595